ROSS RICHIE Chief Executive Officer • **MATT GAGNON** Editor-in-Chief • **FILIP SABLIK** VP-Publishing & Marketing • **LANCE KREITER** VP-Licensing & Merchandising • **PHIL BARBARO** Director of Finance
BRYCE CARLSON Managing Editor • **DAFNA PLEBAN** Editor • **SHANNON WATTERS** Editor • **ERIC HARBURN** Assistant Editor • **ADAM STAFFARONI** Assistant Editor • **CHRIS ROSA** Assistant Editor
STEPHANIE GONZAGA Graphic Designer • **CAROL THOMPSON** Production Designer • **JASMINE AMIRI** Operations Coordinator • **DEVIN FUNCHES** Marketing & Sales Assistant

CREATED BY
Pendleton Ward
WRITTEN BY
Ryan North

ILLUSTRATED BY
Shelli Paroline
and Braden Lamb

FREE COMIC BOOK DAY EDITION
ILLUSTRATED BY
Mike Holmes
COLORS BY STUDIO PARLAPÁ

LETTERS BY
Steve Wands

COVER BY
Shelli Paroline
and Braden Lamb

EDITOR   ASSISTANT EDITOR
Shannon Watters   Adam Staffaroni
DESIGNER
Stephanie Gonzaga

With special thanks to
Marisa Marionakis, Rick Blanco, Curtis Lelash, Laurie
Halal-Ono, Keith Mack, Kelly Crews and the wonderful folks
at Cartoon Network.

FOUR DAYS AFTER THE LICH ESCAPED THE BAG OF HOLDING IN **ADVENTURE TIME** ISSUE #1...

I want to be the best BMO I can be, Princess! I want to be the best BMO.

You are the best BMO!

No, because sometimes, I have made little mistakes.

Aw, we all make mistakes!

PFFFT

BMO

See? I make mistakes too: I grabbed the wrong milk. This isn't from cows!

You... drink from cows?

Yeah, sometimes.

But I am a computer, Princess! I was programmed to be perfect.

...I think?

Well, what do you want to be perfect at?

I WANT TO BE PERFECT AT FIGHTS!!

But I don't even know how to start them. How do you know when it's time for fights, Princess?

Come on, you don't want to start fights!

I want to punch bad guys!!

BAD GUY! Take punch 1!

And here's punch 2!

I HAVE PUNCHES 3 THROUGH 65,535 ALREADY PREPARED, BAD GUY!!

But I would never punch you, Princess.

Aw, BMO. I'd never punch you either.

Well, if you really want to get good at fights, you should TRAIN!

I should... train?

Choo choo!

...HEAD!

Ha ha ha!

WHUMPH

CRUNCH

That was awesome, dude.

Heh. I thought you might like it!

But Jake, I can't do crazy messed up things with my head like that!

That's true. Jake, can you fight without your powers?

I dunno. Probably?

No powers! No powers!

Okay Finn, punch me again! I won't use my powers when I block it, honest.

Here it comes!

PUNCH

OW OW OW OW OW OW OW!

Maybe physical fighting isn't your thing, BMO! There are other ways you can fight: passive-aggressively, intellectually, with words, or--

Words! BMO can fight with words!!

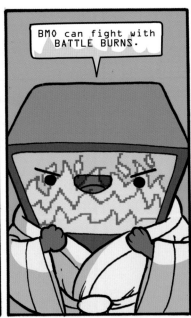

BMO can fight with BATTLE BURNS.

What are battle burns?

I will teach you! Try to punch me!

Okay!

Battle burns are when you're punching me and I say...

ahem

CENSORED DUE TO BMO'S BATTLE BURN BEING SO GOOD, IT CAN'T LEGALLY BE RELEASED TO THE GENERAL PUBLIC!!

BMO, THAT WAS AMAZING!

Nice!

My mind, she is blown!

Can you teach us... battle burns??

I'd love to use them at the royal court!!

To do a battle burn, you need to think of the punches you'd like to punch, and then turn them all into words instead!

You mean up in my brain? I mean, up in my skull walnut?

Correct, Finn!

Hmm...

No punching...

Your sense of style is disagreeable to my aesthetic tastes.

This is hard, BMO!

Is it like when I'm punching someone's head off so it flies up into the sky, and I say something like "Heads up"? Or "Here, I'll give you a HEAD START"?

No! No Finn, that's not a burn at all! Those are puns, that's totally different!

I can see this is going to take a lot of work.

Okay, imagine that YOUR feelings...are actually the feelings of the person you are fighting!

That's just crazy enough to work!!

And now, try to hurt those feelings!

Jake, I think if you applied yourself harder you could accomplish some really amazing things.

Thank you dude; I believe the same.

No, no, no! Princess, can you help them?

Finn! Jake! When I look at you, my eyes show me some reasonable-looking dudes...

...because they know that the slightest comprehension of your actual faces would be to gaze into THE UNBLINKING EYE OF MADNESS!!

Hooray! Princess you have graduated from Level 1 of my class!

Nothing personal, guys.

I've got to get back to Official Princess Business, but this has been a lot of fun. I'll keep practicing!

Bye Princess! Thank you for the cookies!

Why can't you both be more like my star pupil?

I think she's just naturally good at battle burns!

I think she's just naturally good at not being bad at things.

Thanks for teaching us all about battle burns, BMO! I'm sure they'll come in handy.

You need to keep practicing! Tomorrow morning!

I know!

And I will keep practicing my body slams too. When you fall asleep tonight I am going to try to body slam you, Finn!

Awesome.

This has been a really wonderful weekend.

It has, hasn't it? I don't think anything could happen now to ruin it.

It is not possible for **ANYTHING** and/or **ANYONE** to ruin this weekend, dude!

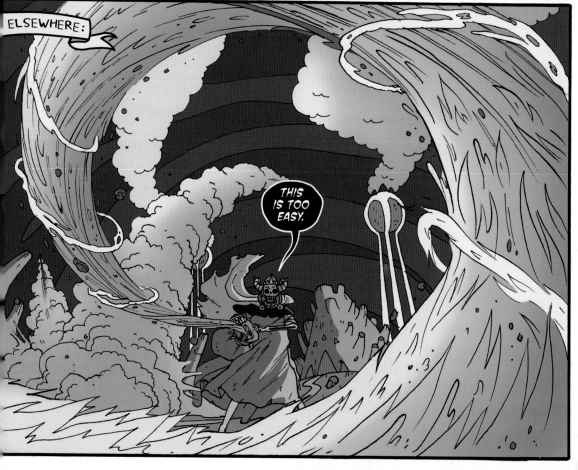

ELSEWHERE:

THIS IS TOO EASY.

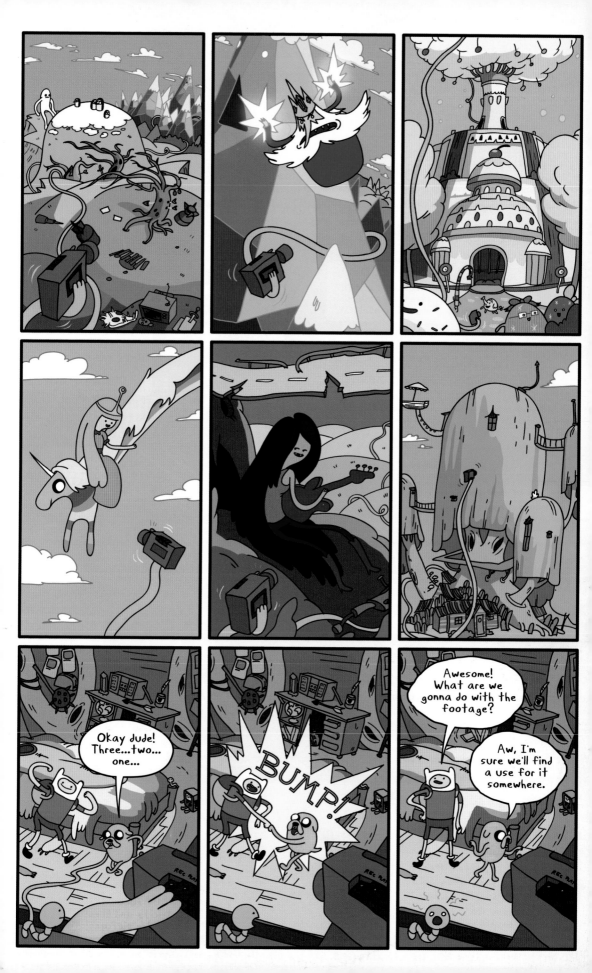

ADVENTURE TIME

Jake the Dog: Magical dog with stretchy powers. Pal rating at 110%!

Finn the Human: Awesome dude with awesome hat. Pal rating at 110%!

The Land of Ooo: A pretty magical place! Jake and Finn live here. Adventure possibility: UNLIMITED??

Really good at being pals **AND** at adventures!

Ice King: All he wants to do is marry a princess, and he thinks stealing them is okay!

The Lich: HE IS COMING.

Marceline the Vampire Queen: Over a thousand years old. Be cool, okay?

Princess Bubblegum: Human/bubblegum ruler of the Candy Kingdom. She's made of gum! She and Finn are friends, and sometimes feelings can get complicated, you know?

Not as important as the other boxes, just a heads up.

Written by **Ryan North** Art by **Shelli Paroline** and **Braden Lamb** "Adventure Time" created by **Pendleton Ward**

BMO runs on electricity and likes taking nice pictures!

Not pictured is the **EARL OF LEMONGRAB**, who is currently sitting in a chair in an empty room, screaming.

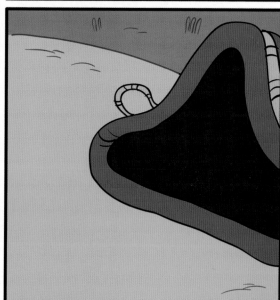

Uh oh.

There's another sign just out of frame that says, "Look at this workmanship and I'm sure you'll see / Ain't nobody better at making quick, extremely accurate signs than me

FIVE DAYS LATER:

Okay dude, try this one on for size!

"Your mom called...!"

"She said it was time to go home and stop bothering us. She said she has to talk to you THROUGH US because she's so ashamed."

Sweet!!

But scope this:

"You call THAT a 'punch'? Because it seems more just like WATERED-DOWN FRUIT JUICE! It's disappointing, and makes me sad."

Huh. I don't think that was a very good battle burn.

Hey man, I appreciate your honesty.

KRAKA-DOOM

Was that YOU?

Uncool, Lich.

You know what we gotta do, buddy...

Found them!

Asymptotic!

Slant asymptotic, dude!

I knew it was cool for a dude to keep anti-mind-control jewelry around the house.

Man, you know I don't judge. I kinda like wearing jewelry too sometimes.

We can talk about that later...

...because right now we've got an **EVIL LICH** to beat!!

Whoa!

He's headed towards the Candy Kingdom! **WE'VE GOT TO SAVE PRINCESS BUBBLEGUM!**

And everyone else who lives there too!

We've got to slow him down! Use a battle burn!

HEY, *LICH!* YOUR HANDS ARE SO *SKELETON*-Y AND *GROSS* THAT I BET NOBODY *EVER* WANTS TO HOLD YOUR HAND! I BET THAT MAKES YOU FEEL *BAD* WHEN YOU REALLY THINK ABOUT IT!!

I think you hurt his feelings, dude!

Totally worth it!!

BUMP!!

Man, there sure are some cool things buried in the dirt. I refer both to this comic book page AND to real life in general.

FOOLS. I WILL SUCK EVERYTHING YOU'VE EVER KNOWN INTO THIS BAG AND THEN I WILL THROW IT INTO THE SUN. DO YOU REALLY THINK A BOY AND HIS BLOBBY DOG CAN STOP ME?

Yeah, we do!

THEN WATCH. WATCH AS YOUR PLANET DIES.

NEVER!

This is serious, dude. This is a real end-of-the-world scenario. I think we both know what we have to...nay, GET to do.

I hear you, man. Let's DO THIS!

Ready?

Ready!

JAAAAAAKE SUUUUUUUUUUUUIT!

Have you tried **NOT** sucking for a change, Lich?!

KA-POW

HA HA HA!

What are you laughing for? I Punched you into two pieces!

And you should quit now, while you're **A HEAD!**

BUMP!

I DON'T THINK I WILL.

LOOK: YOU'RE WASTING YOUR TIME.

PRINCESS BUBBLEGUM!

And everyone else who lives there tooooo!

AND NOW, YOU.

NO!

NOOOOOOOOOO!

I don't think he can hear us in here, dude.

Where are we?! Where's the way out? The Lich's butt isn't going to kick itself!

WE NEED TO HELP IT DO THAT, JAKE!!

Huh.

Maybe she knows?

Gentlemen! Hello!

Hello, your highness! I'm Jake the Dog, and this is my friend, Finn the Human. We're going to stop The Lich! He's uh, a skeleton dude. I think? It's gross. I dunno.

He's a gross jerk!!

I think we may have something in common, gentlemen, for it was **THAT VERY SAME GROSS JERK** who sent me here! Greetings Finn and Jake, and welcome to my kingdom.

I'm Desert Princess.

And it is very nice to meet you!!

SHAKE SHAKE

SHAKE

SHAKE

SHAKE

SHAKE

Hey, you sure you're not DESSERT Princess?

No, I'm Desert Princess. It's on account of how I'm really good at sand. You wanna see?

Yes please!

Okay, almost...

Almoooost...

PSAMMO!

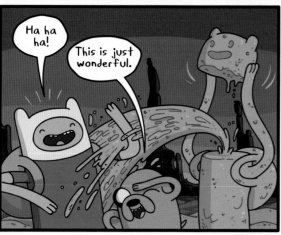

Ha ha ha!

This is just wonderful.

I don't think that'll really help us escape though.

You know any way out of this bag, Princess?

No, and I haven't met anyone else! I think everyone who gets sucked in ends up somewhere different...

But there's gotta be SOMETHING we can punch to escape!

I don't really see anything around here that needs punching, man.

I'm afraid I don't see anything either, Mister Finn. I think we may be trapped here...

FOREVER.

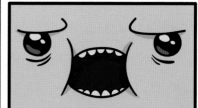

We must've stayed together on our way into the bag because we were in Jake Suit mode!

I love Jake Suit, dude.

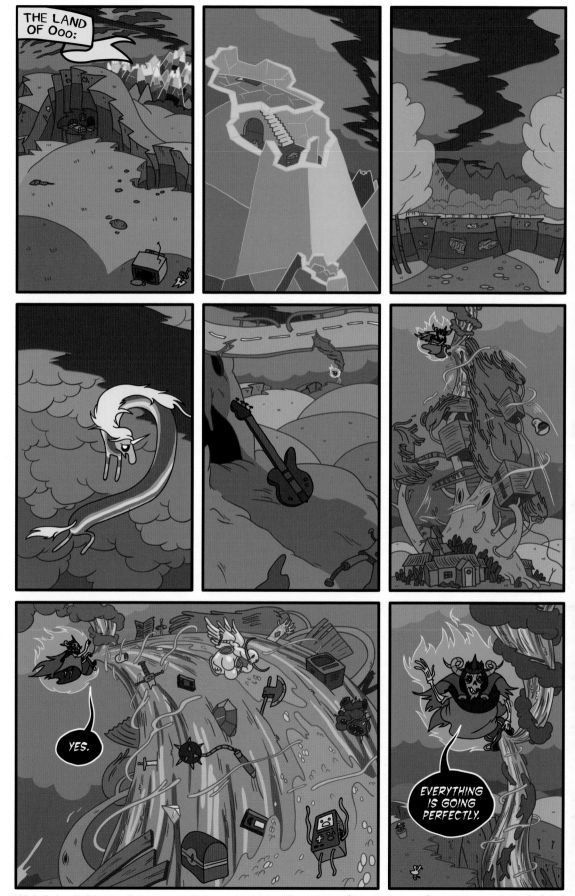

While in the bag, BMO has an entirely awesome, entirely separate adventure. The particulars of this adventure are left open to your imagination/fan fiction.

The Lich!

Marceline's house!

What now?

If this were an audio comic you could hear what Marceline was playing and, faced with hearing such beauty, your ears would weep.

INSIDE THE LICH'S BAG!

Man, if we don't find a way out soon the entire world is doomed!

We really should've saved the day by now, Jake.

Maybe this **IS** our world now, buddy. We could live right here!

You know... settle down, make ourselves a nice sand house to live in--no! A sand **CASTLE!** After all, Desert Princess lives here and she does all right.

Yes sir!

How long did you say you've lived here, DP?

I can't rightly say, Mister Finn! My earliest memory is of being sucked up by the Lich near some sort of...Candied Kingdom.

Hmm.

But it's blurry...**ALMOST** like I saw it from several different perspectives at once, as a bunch of candy citizens were smooshed together to form a new entity! But ha ha that's crazy!

Hmm...

Then I woke up here! Anyone as fancy as me is **CLEARLY** a princess, and I realized this has got to be my kingdom!

HMM...!

I ACCEPT YOUR VERSION OF EVENTS.

Desert Princess is as mysterious as she is...made out of desserts.

But I still think we need to escape this bag, Jake.

AW MAN!

How come we ALWAYS have to save the world JUST as I finish up the best castle eve--

--nevermind let's go.

Well. Maybe we should search that-a-way?

ON IT, Princess. WHAT TIME IS IT??

ADDDDVENTURE TIME!!

Time to escape this bag!!

Oh, I didn't know you two had your own thing going.

Sorry.

What time is it??

AD VENTURE TIME!

FINN AND JAKE'S ADVERTISING CORPORATION

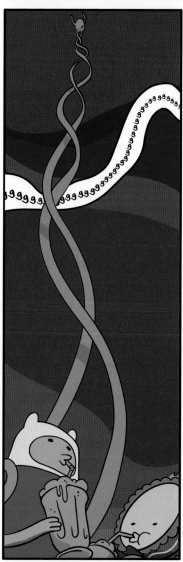

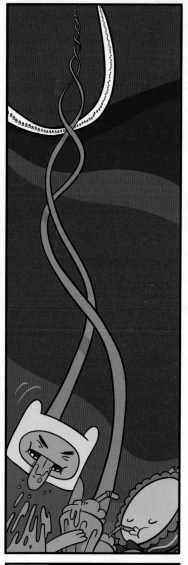

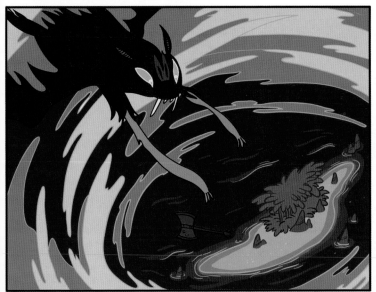

As soon as I get out of here, **SOMEONE**'s gonna get their butt kicked!

Obvs!

Who's there?! Hynden, is that you?

No, Marceline, it's me.

Wow. Way to dress, Bonnibel.

Royal dresses are too warm for the beach! Don't be mean!

So, you know a way off this island?

Maybe. What else can you turn into, besides bats and wolves and monsters?

I can also turn into a tentacle monster.

HOW DOES THAT HELP OUR SITUATION?

HOW DOES IT HURT OUR SITUATION, THOUGH?

ELSEWHERE IN THE BAG:

Dude! I didn't find a way out, but I **DID** see the Ice King nearby!! You wanna go mess with him?

He might know a way out of here!

Yeah, we should probably go mess with him.

Hey! Stop whatever you're doing!!

Oh, hey guys. You got bagged too, huh? It's pretty sucky here, am I right?

Ice King! You're evil, and I'm pretty sure you know a way out of here!

Hey, great to see you too, **FRIEND.** Look, I got nothing to do with this. I got sucked up just like everyone else, only I landed alone without Gunter **OR** my fan fiction.

Aw, that's awful. Hi there--I'm Desert Princess.

Thank you! Nice to get some empathy for once. These two only give me punches all up in my face.

Is that true?

He deserves it a lot of the time.

Is **THAT** true?

SHRUG

 "Greetings, Jake!!!" said cake, stretching herself to form the words "Greetings, Jake!!!"

Ice King, if you wouldn't mind?

My pleasure, Princess.

Sure you don't want a sand-cheese and sand-cucumber sand-wich, Finn?

Naw, I'm good.

Your loss, dude.

Do you guys know why Gunter and my fictions didn't land here with me?

Nope! You're actually the first person we've seen here, besides Desert Princess.

Maybe we should ask why YOU landed so close to US!

Hmm...

Maybe--maybe it's because I'm... JOINED with you guys somehow? Our destinies somehow COSMICALLY INTER-TWINED?

Nuh-uh! If that were true then how come Princess Bubblegum or Flame Princess isn't here too?

I dunno, man. I think that's a question only your heart can answer.

My... heart?

Is this some sort of...metaphorical language relying on an ancient cultural misunderstanding of the heart being the center of emotion??

MEANWHILE, OUTSIDE THE BAG:

I can't even believe I used to live here, Melissa. I could just **DIE.**

Everything's gross here. You have to promise not to tell Brad I ever lived like this.

OH MY GLOB Melissa I gotta go!

There's this skeleton guy and he's sucking up all my stuff! I'm serious Melissa, he's sucking up my **LUMPING HOUSE!**

No I don't know him, Melissa. **NO!** No way I'm asking him that, **MELISSA.** I'm telling you, he's gross. **HE'S GROSS!**

ARRRRGGGH!

Crust

Upper mantle

Mantle

Earth's outer core (liquid nickel and iron)

Bad news for every living thing on the planet

ALMOST DONE.

I, THE TALKY ONE, REGRET TALKING SO MUCH.

Let's learn more about the Earth's crust! As you may have heard, yes, it is mainly made out of old crusts.

Melissa? **MELISSA!** Skeleton guy made me say all that junk!

Zero bars?! I hate this lumping phone!

SPLAT

Hey there, guys.

Ugh.

Dudes, we're not making any progress on saving the world here!! In fact, we're making **NEGATIVE** progress, because now Lumpy Space Princess is here and all we've done is **HAVE A PICNIC!**

Though it was very nice of you to make it for us, Desert Princess.

I made the ice!

Thank you.

What do you want us to do, man? We've looked on the ground **AND** in the sky! There's nowhere else to look, unless somehow we could tunnel through the ground itself with some sort of amazing d--

AMAZING DRILL HANDS!!

To be fair, it's extremely hard NOT to hate a lumping phone with zero bars.

BUMP

How come the tunnel is lit when there's no torches? It's the same way the inside of the bag is lit when there's no sun: SCIENCE. Wait no hold on wait wait I meant to say MAGIC.

Where?

Over there! But we're not gonna get there if you're not the sail.

Fine, jeez. Bossy much?

Marcy, I'm the SKIPPER.

SOON:

I could use some help!

SORRY! TOO BUSY BEING THE SAIL HERE, SKIP!

What do you think Finn and Jake are up to?

Aw, they're probably beating bad guys up as we speak. I'm sure we've got nothing to worry about.

What the cabbage?

PRINCESS BUBBLEGUM! PRINCESS BUBBLEGUM!! OH MY GLOB IT'S TERRIBLE! IT'S SO SAD!

Ladies, I don't really know how to say this, but...well--

FINN AND JAKE ARE TOTALLY DEAD!!

HA HA HA YES!

Thank you for going on this journey with us! This is...

The End

 with Finn & Jake

was
Written by **Ryan North**
Art was done by **Shelli Paroline** and **Braden Lamb**
was Lettered by **Steve Wands**
"Adventure Time" created by **Pendleton Ward**

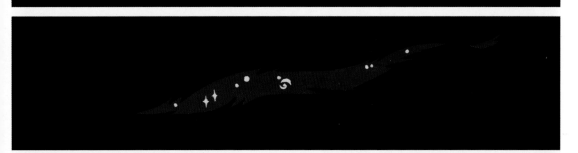

Sorry we're late! Here's the **KNUCKLE SANDWICH** you ordered!

I DIDN'T--

I meant it **METAPHORICALLY!!**

PUNCH PUNCH

What have you done with Ooo? Why are we in space?!

PUNCH PUNCH

TELL HIM, JAKE.

Um...I think he really did suck up the entire planet into his bag?

YES.

AND ALL THAT REMAINS IS THIS LAST...

Hey! Don't say "little"!

...LITTLE...

If you say "bit" I'm coming back to kick your butt! I'ma shoot missiles in your face; I'm not even joking!

...BIT.

ELSEWHERE:

I saw them die with my own LUMPIN' EYES!

Their last words were "I ask only that Princess Bubblegum and the Ice King get married, that would be quite..." Drat, what's that word Finn says? Um, "Rad."

No, wait! "Mathematical"!

That's not true, Princess. Finn and Jake's last words were "This isn't part of the plan!" and then they were gone.

Those aren't much better.

That's what *I* thought!

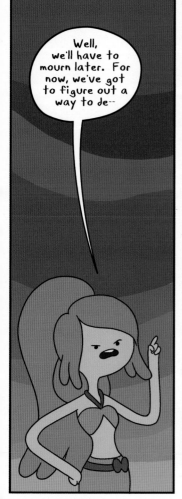

Well, we'll have to mourn later. For now, we've got to figure out a way to de--

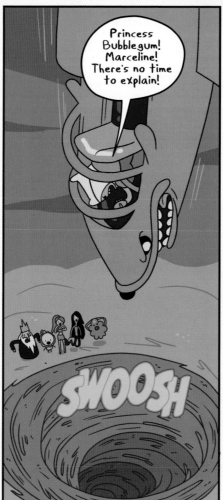

Princess Bubblegum! Marceline! There's no time to explain!

SWOOSH

That's okay, it's clear what's going on!

Alternate, worse line for Princess Bubblegum: "That's okay, it's PLANE what's going on!" (because of Jet Jake) (did you know: not all puns are good?!)

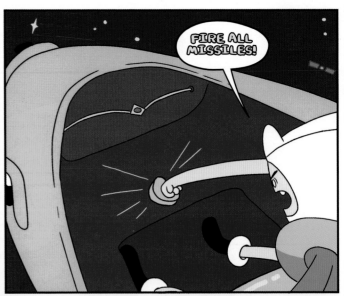

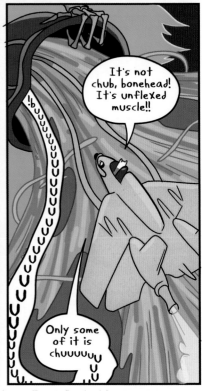

Jet Jake moves in space the same way spaceships move in space: by expelling gas (i.e.: toots)

That didn't go nearly as well as it did in my imagination.

Tell me about it, man! In my imagination his head exploded.

Listen, can you do me a favor on the way down? Think of a way we can beat him while he's got that stupid bag protecting him, okay?

On it!

SOON:

So now you're up to speed with everything that's happened with us so far!

Thank you, Jake.

Hey, don't mention it.

Guys! Princesses! Vampire Queen! I know how we can beat the Lich!!

It's like Abraham Lincoln once said in the past and also on Mars! I just have to believe in myself. We just have to believe in ourselves! In **ALL** of ourselves!!

What does that even **MEAN**, Finn?

WE WORK TOGETHER! HOLD ON! USUALLY IT'S EASIER FOR ME TO TALK IF I'M NOT SHOUTING ACROSS A VORTEX!

We all have our special skills, right? We should attack together! Look at us: **I'M** good at punches; Princess Bubblegum's super smart; Jake can take the shape of anything he can imagine--

Heh. Yeah.

--Desert Princess can make sand people; Marceline, you're a real-life vampire; Ice King can make giant ice cubes to hold people in--

There's more to me than just my ice powers, Finn. I hope you one day realize that.

And Lumpy Space Princess, you...well, um, you can--

Oh my glob, Finn, it's **SUPER** obvious, I should just bite him. You know, give him a case of the Lumps.

LSP, that's **PERFECT!** As soon as he gets lumpy he won't care about destroying us anymore!

But how can we attack him all at once when he can control our minds? We don't have enough anti-mind-control gems for everybody.

We...

...form...

...TEAMS!!

Some people say they prefer working alone to working in groups, but I bet that's just because they've never had Finn propose a team to them before!

AWESOME!

It's been a sl-ICE!

Man, that didn't make sense. You're not even attacking with a sword!

Oh wait, I get ittttttttttt

You want some science in your face??

It appears he didn't want science in OR about his face, Princess.

Hey Lich! Looks like you've got to TAKE YOUR LUMPS!

OW! He's just skin and bones and I lumpin' bit myself!!

Like I need more lumpin' LUMPS!

My crown protects me from the Lich's mind control!

Mine too!

High five?

If I high five you, will you try to kidnap me?

Ye-um, I mean, uh...there's one way to find out?

We're not making much progress here, Finn. We're running out of time.

The Lich said he'd suck everything up and then throw it into the sun. So, uh, how long do you think that would take?

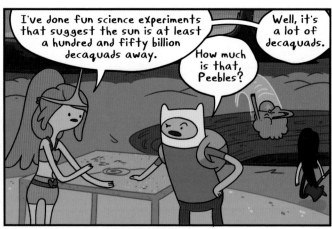

I've done fun science experiments that suggest the sun is at least a hundred and fifty billion decaquads away.

How much is that, Peebles?

Well, it's a lot of decaquads.

We've managed to keep the Lich too busy fighting us to finish the job...for now. But if he does throw us into the sun it should take us at least a couple of years to get there, unless he can somehow throw us mad nutty hard. But to get such force levels you'd need to--

Oh great, that's plenty of time then!

Yes--except the closer we get to the sun, the hotter things will get. It won't take long for it to be too hot for us to survive!

How long until it's too hot for sweet hats?

I'm gonna say..."soon."

gasp

Three things. One: this isn't working. Two: I don't know how much longer we can keep this up. Three: that guy is the worst.

HOW! COME! WE!

KEEP NOT WINNING?!

SOON:

Alright everybody, new plan: we form one giant **SUPER ULTIMATE TEAM** instead! Desert Princess, I need you to make all the Sand Finns **AND** Sand Jakes you can. I want a Sand Bro Army!

Yes sir! I could also make sand Liches, sand witches, and sandwiches if you want!

Just the last one, please!

Ice King, you make Snow Finns too! Make all the snow guys you can! They'll be teaming up with the sand ones.

There's not much moisture in the air so it might be tric--

Ice King **DO YOU WANT EVERYONE TO DIE??**

Okay, well no, not really I guess--

Lumpy Space Princess, you'll tell the Sand and Snow Bros what a jerk the Lich is, so they'll **REALLY** want to punch him. They'll be a little slow since they don't have brains, but that'll stop them from being mind-controlled!

That's easy, 'cause I've got lots of stories about him that you don't even know. I mean, that guy tried to mess up my **RELATIONSHIPS.**

Princess Bubblegum, you'll stay here to organize the army and make sure they go in on my mark. Marceline, you're tough and awesome, so you keep fighting the Lich while we get ready in here.

Not a problem.

What about me, Finn? Isn't there something ol' Jake gets to do?

Yes. My friend, you've got the **MOST IMPORTANT JOB OF ALL!!** And here it is!

PSS PSS PSS PSS PSS PSS

Hee hee! That tickles!

Cool plan though.

SOON:

This is really appealing to me for some reason.

I know what you mean, dude.

And then he calls me "talky," and it's like, YEAH, at least I've got something worth saying!!

Looks like we're ready here, Finn.

Alright. Put your gem on, Jake.

Oh, it's ON.

Ha, I didn't even mean that in the "let's go fight" sense! It totally works though.

Heh. Crazy.

I've ordered the first wave of Elemental Finns and Jakes to follow you in, Finn!

Perfect! We're going in!!

Marceline! Remember you promised to give me back my crown in one piece!

— Don't get hurt.

Good luck or whatever, Finn. I mean it. I'm being serious.

And good luck, Mr. Jake.

And good luck, M--

And Ice King? Good luck to Ice King? Hello?

See ya Princesses!

You suck me in your bag, man, you know I'm coming back!

If I were you right now I'd have anxiety ATTACKS!

You dumb to do something again, expectin' different things to happen!

The only thing that changed is that we all just started RAPPIN'!

We're gonna end this soon, Lich.

So don't you even blink!

We're gonna see what happens when I...

NO!

...start to...

NO!!

...SHRINK!

RIIIIP

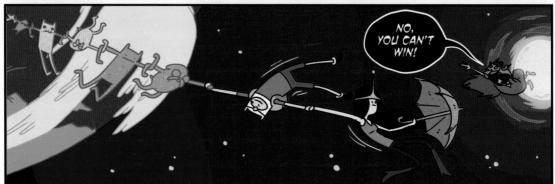

EARTH:

Hey. Thanks for keeping The Lich busy while we fought him, sand and ice Finns and Jakes.

Hey, um...was the planet always shaped like that?

Hopefully, dude!!

Listen, we should get back down there. I think there're still some problems that need fixing.

I agree. You two are with me.

Wooooosh!

Woooosh!

Stop making wooshy noises, guys.

Woooooosh no way this is awesome wooooosh

Princess Bubblegum! What happened?

I was about to ask you the same thing!

Did you get him?

Well, I GUESS you could say The Lich should've worn a wide-brimmed hat today, because he's spending an awful lot of time...

IN THE SUN.

Yes, we got him. We were lucky to escape ourselves.

Thank you, Marceline. We all owe each of you a debt of gratitude.

Here, thanks for lending me your hat.

Marceline! It's a ROYAL CROWN.

BUMP

So listen, what's with all the dirt everywhere?

I have no idea! But it's all over the Candy Kingdom.

Weird! When we were hanging out in **SPACE ITSELF**, everything looked all deserty and desertlicious from there too.

Are you saying the sand covers the entire **PLANET?!**

I think so? Probably? I guess?

Oh no!

When the bag broke, we all ended up back where we started. But that desert kingdom was already there in the bag before we showed up!

So?

So the bag changed it somehow! Instead of ending up wherever it started, it ended up on top of us. On top of **EVERYTHING!**

Does Desert Princess know anything about this?

Nobody's seen her since the bag exploded!

Jake and I accept your quest, Princess! We will find Desert Princess and restore this land to its rightful, non-sandy state!

Aw, man! Dude.

We just got back, dude.

Can you restore the Breakfast Kingdom too? All the breakfast citizens have sand in them. It's gross.

Yes! We'll restore **ALL** the kingdoms!

Aw man! **THAT'S EVEN MORE WORK THAN THE FIRST QUEST!**

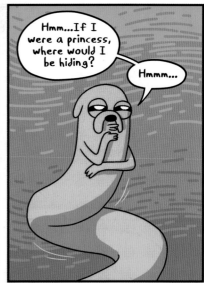

Wha--?

Gentlemen! I knew you'd come!

The Ice King is about to apologize to you, Princess!

I am?

Hooray!

Yeah man! It's what you're supposed to do after being a big patoot!

But I'm NEVER a big patoot!!

Oh wait!

I guess sometimes I am.

I'm sorry I kidnapped you, Princess.

Well. You should be.

Don't you have better things to do than kidnap people? Maybe you'd want to, I don't know, GET RID OF ALL THAT SAND COVERING YOUR KINGDOM?

That's REAL?

I thought it was just a new form of ice; "crunchy ice that tastes bad in my drinks and also fails to cool them"?

I just assumed I was seeing things! The sand goes on forever, Finn. There's got to be enough there to...

...to fill in a giant hole?!

...I was gonna say "feed an army" but sure.

WAIT, THAT'S IT! All we have to do is take all the sand covering the world and stick it in that giant hole!

Yes, Jake?

How are we gonna do that, dude? The planet is huge and there's sand everywhere!

I have an idea, Mr. Finn!

What if I used some sand to make a sand version of...myself? Then Sand Me could make another Sand Me, and so on!

Then they all just walk into the hole and jump in!

I've never done a sand version of myself before, but it should work. Right?

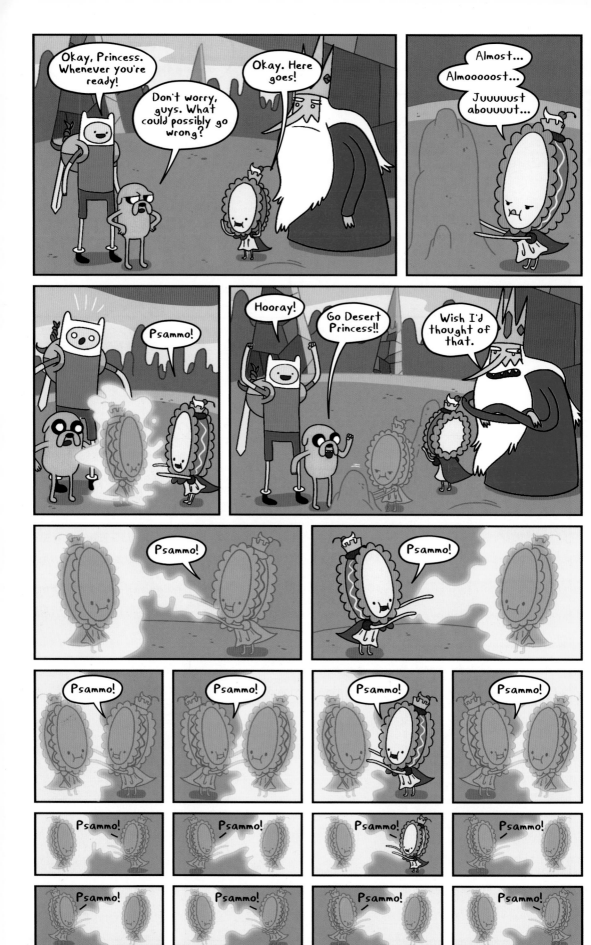

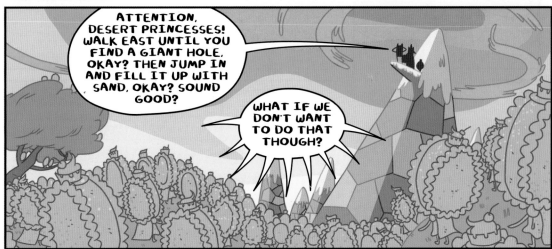

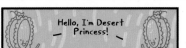

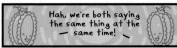

WHAT IF--AND THIS IS EMBARRASSING BUT, WELL, WHAT IF WE ALL HAVE A BIT OF A CRUSH ON YOU, FINN?

You guys!! Don't say that!

BUT IT'S TRUE.

AND WE DON'T WANT TO DISAPPEAR WITHOUT GETTING ONE LITTLE FINN KISS.

Oh my gosh oh my gosh this is so embarrassing!

But I can't kiss all of you! There's way too many. I'll get all puckered out!

NOT A PROBLEM, MISTER FINN.

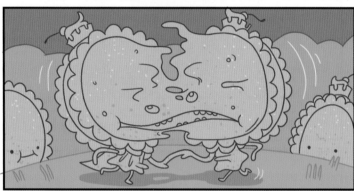

Welp, I'm out. That's my limit of crazy for today!

Um... ha ha

SOON:

Filling in that hole has given us a whole new land to explore! You've literally given us a larger planet to live on, Finn! This is amazing.

Well shoot, Desert Princess did most of the work! I just had to kiss some sand.

Thank you, Desert Princess.

Thank **YOU**, Princess Bubblegum.

Alright! Water Princess, we could use a lake!

You know, I'm really glad I got to meet you, Desert Princess.

I'm--
I'm really glad I got to meet you too, Mister Finn.

Please. All my friends just call me "Finn".

THE END

Drawn by
Shelli and Braden

Written by
Ryan

Created by
Pen

 Thanks for reading!

ONE THOUSAND YEARS AGO:

Whoa, check this place out!! And it even comes with a cool creepy bag! I could **TOTALLY** stay here until it's safe outside again.

Actually, I don't--I don't think I like this. It feels weird. It's kinda burning my hand.

Maybe I shouldn't be here after all.

Marcy, I know the mushroom bombs have...changed things. Awakened...things. And I know I've been alone for so long that I've started talking to myself.

But don't be afraid, Marceline! We're tough! We're smart!

We'll make it through this. I promise.

It's fine. There'll be somewhere else to stay. Somewhere else where we can find...friends. Besides, it can't stay like this forever, right?

...

Everything is gonna be fine.

It'll just take some time.

My Cider the Mountain

Why, hello Princess Bubblegum! I got the cider I made for Cinnamon Bun's birthday party right here!

Huh? OH!

I thought I canceled that order, Tree Trunks!

I pressed it from the ELUSIVE Subrosa Sweet! My FAVORITE APPLE!

Are you EVEN LISTENING, Tree Trunks? I CANCELED THAT ORDER!

WHAT?! WHY? I thought you and Cinnamon Bun LIKED it!

HAHA! I did, but I LOVE the MYSTERIOUS CIDER from the SKY!

Cider from the...

Here comes a batch NOW!

Aw CRUMBS!

No matter... Someone get Cinnamon Bun to mop up this MESS! CHOP!CHOP!

CLAP!

CLAP! CLAP! CLAP!

WELL, where is he?! I can't mop it up! I need to... um... choose the NAPKINS! The party is TONIGHT!

The cider is very good... but it tastes ...FAMILIAR.

Farewell y'all! Princess Bubblegum, I'll miss you!

Okay! Sure! See you!

At least the forest critters still like my cider...

SNAP!

WHAT WAS THAT?!

Maybe this was a bad ide–OH!

Cider! I was RIGHT! That creature IS the other cider maker!

That FLAVOR! It uses the Subrosa Sweet! I'm sure of it! But it's also got a ... MUSKY ... almost CINNAMON aftertaste...

Tree Trunks!

Cinnamon Bun?!?

YOU'RE THE MYSTERIOUS CIDER MAKER?! WHY?

I don't know what'cher sayin', Tree Trunks!

You're makin' CIDER! UP HERE ON THE MOUNTAIN!!!

NO I AIN'T! I be DRINKIN' it up!

I'm on a JUICE CLEANSE!

Cupcake got me a stay here at this spa for my birthday!

Hmm...

COVER GALLERY

Cover 1D:
Jeffrey Brown

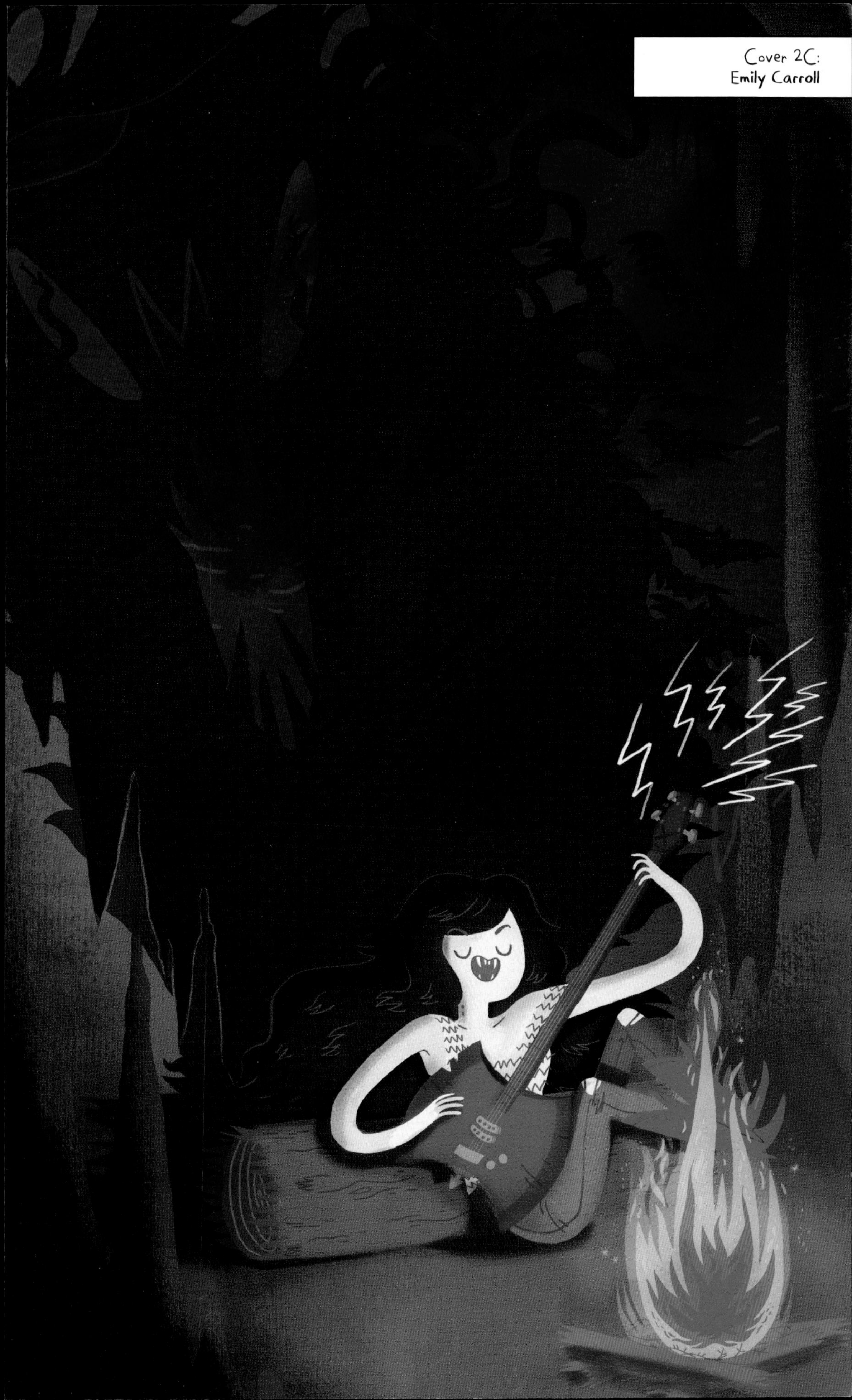

Cover 2C:
Emily Carroll

Cover 3C:
Michael DeForge

Cover 3D:
Stephanie Buscema

Cover 4B:
Kassandra Heller

Kassandra
HELLER

Cover 4C:
Scott C.